Approaching Christmas

Meditations for Advent

Joyce Huggett

D1395599

A LION BOOK
Tring · Batavia · Sydney

For Bob
and in memory of Betty

Introduction

'Dear God,
I like Christmas because it's your birthday.
Most people like Christmas because of the presents.'
Dennis

I don't know who Dennis is except that his letter appears in the book *Children's Letters to God*. What I do know is that Dennis has summed up my feelings about Christmas in a delightfully concise and refreshing way.

I love Christmas. I love receiving Christmas cards and sending out a newsletter to our many friends. I love choosing and wrapping up presents. I love decorating the church with holly and ivy in preparation for the Carol Service. And, on Christmas Eve, I love to dress the family Christmas tree while I listen to a service of carols and readings on the radio.

All the preparations and paraphernalia which are part and parcel of the countdown to Christmas – the smell of spices when I make the Christmas puddings, icing the Christmas cake – never cease to delight me. And yet, as the years wear on, the big build-up to Christmas irritates me too. These festivities are such fun, so absorbing and so time-consuming that they can easily detract from the real reason for the festivities: the celebration on Christmas Day of the most stupendous event that ever took place in the world's history – the birth of God's Son.

A few years ago, I determined that I would not allow the commercialization of Christmas to crowd out its true meaning. Instead, I would hold two things in tension. While still enjoying the celebrations, I would also make time each day to marvel at how, on the first Christmas Day, the invisible, intangible God made himself visible and tangible in the babe of Bethlehem. I would meditate on some Bible passages which highlight these truths and then respond in prayer.

I decided to start my meditations on Advent Sunday – four Sundays before Christmas Day. Traditionally, for many Christians, Advent reminds us that, just as Jesus once came to this earth as a tiny baby, so he has promised to return one day – but this time he will not come in vulnerability but as a conquering King. The Bible passages on this theme thrill me and remind me of the need to prepare for this Second Coming of Christ even more diligently than I prepare to celebrate his birthday.

Advent Sunday came and, as usual, I lit my Advent candle, read the Bible passages and reflected on them. Then I searched for photographs or pictures which would illustrate what I had read and stuck them in a photograph album, alongside each passage. I also typed out any quotations from commentaries and books which helped to deepen my understanding of these passages. And I made my personal response by adding a prayer of my own. As the days went on, I realized that something profound was happening. I was still enjoying the pre-Christmas preparations to the full, but at the same time, as I spent time with God, I was grasping, in a fresh way, the depth and the length and the breadth and the height of his love. I was being filled with a deeper excitement and joy.

That year, I really began to appreciate the three parts of the good news of Advent:

Christ came
Christ comes
Christ will come

For a few days I looked at the future: *Christ will come.* Then I turned my attention to the present: *Christ comes.* Then, as Christmas Day drew closer, I focused my attention on the old, yet ever-new story of the first Christmas. As the Christmas cards arrived, I selected some for my book of meditations.

I still have that original book. I still use it during Advent, through Christmas and into the New Year when the church traditionally celebrates Epiphany – the time when we think of the visit of the wise men. It helps me to focus on Jesus. I know many people who long, as I do, to focus on the Christ of Christmas and think of how God stooped down and became *Emmanuel* – God with us.

For this reason, I have put together here some of the Bible readings which I have used, as well as a meditation or a thought, a hymn or a prayer for the time of Advent and Christmas. My longing is that those who want to focus on the meaning of Christmas will take time each day to be still, to turn to this book, and find Jesus Christ entering their lives in a new and vital way. On that Advent Sunday when I resolved to keep Christ central to my Christmas, I wrote this prayer:

Still at last, dear Lord,
I come to you,
Weary from the busyness of a thousand things which
clamour for attention
But longing to feel your touch afresh
This Christmastime.
Kindle in me
A love for you
which finds time for you
which responds to you
which yearns for your return.
Cause my heart to leap for joy
As I anticipate that great fact of the future –
Your re-entry to earth.
Pour into me the certainty that believes
That all life is to be lived under the shadow
Of that miraculous return,
The courage to live life your way
And the resilience to hold on to that hope
When times are hard
Or my body tired.
Bring me to Christmas Day
Not irritated with the commercialization with which
it is surrounded
But rather, rejoicing in the message of the angels

To me
Today
Is born
My Saviour

Hallelujah

He's coming back!

One December morning a Christmas card from my brother in Australia dropped through my letter-box. As always, I read his annual letter from the other side of the globe with eagerness. This year it was extra-special: *'Well, folks! Here's the news you've been waiting for! I'm coming home! I've booked my annual leave and bought my air ticket. I'll be arriving in June and I'll be in England for three whole weeks.'*

I read those words over and over again as I considered the implications. So many thoughts rushed through my mind: 'We haven't seen each other for seventeen years! What will the reunion be like? Will we recognize one another after all this time? What will we talk about? What will we do?'

My brother came. We did recognize each other. When we met, at first there were no words to say. We simply held each other in a warm embrace. But after that, we found plenty to say. After all, there were seventeen years of news to catch up on as well as plenty of childhood reminiscences to share.

The good news we focus on in Advent is contained in God's 'letter from home' as St Augustine used to describe the Bible. It is this: Jesus is coming back to take us to be with himself for ever.

'One word of command, one shout from the archangel, one blast from the trumpet of God and the Lord himself will come down from Heaven! Those who have died in Christ will be the first to rise, and then we who are still living on the earth will be swept up with them into the clouds to meet the Lord in the air. And after that we shall be with him for ever. So by all means use this message to encourage one another.'

1 Thessalonians 4:16-18

Lord Jesus, it sometimes seems too good to be true that you really are coming back to take us to be with yourself. At other times, I confess, life here on earth seems so good that I don't want you to come back yet. Forgive me, dear Lord, for my doubting and for my coldness. Fill me with awe this Advent as I contemplate again the mysteries contained in your Word which assure us that you will return and that you want us to be ready. Then give me the resolve to change my life-style so that, no matter when you come, I shall be ready to greet you with joy and thanksgiving. Ready, too, to drop everything to come to you.

Lo! He comes, with clouds descending,
Once for favoured sinners slain;
Thousand thousand saints attending
Swell the triumph of His train;
Hallelujah!
Christ appears on earth to reign.

John Cennick, Charles Wesley and Martin Madan

Come, Lord Jesus!

One evening, while I was on holiday in Cyprus, I sat on the shore of a salt lake and watched the sun set. For nearly an hour, the sun was reflected like a golden ball, in the tranquil lake. As I watched, a black line divided the sun-ball in half. This apparent fissure deepened as the black mountains gradually swallowed up the now-red ball.

An hour later, back at the flat, I was still thinking about the splendour of that sunset. Suddenly, there was a loud bang. The flat began to shudder and the entire neighbourhood was plunged into darkness. An earthquake was shaking the little port. High-rise blocks of flats were swaying like trees in a breeze and countless people were struck with terror.

My mind flashed back to the sunset. And certain prophecies concerning Jesus' return immediately came to mind. 'Perhaps Jesus is about to return – *now*,' I thought.

These strange happenings did not, in fact, herald Jesus' return. Even so, they served to underline, for me, the truth that one day he will come back, not clothed in poverty and humility, as in his first appearance, but resplendent in glory and majesty. He will come in triumph. And everyone will see him.

> 'The sun will be darkened, the moon will fail to give her light, the stars will fall from the sky, and the powers of heaven will be shaken. Then the Son of Man will appear in the sky, and all the nations of the earth will wring their hands as they see the Son of Man coming on the clouds of the sky in power and great splendour. And he will send out his angels with a loud trumpet-call and they will gather together his chosen from the four winds – from one end of the heavens to the other.'
>
> Matthew 24:29-31

Lord Jesus, may we look forward to your Second Coming with anticipation and with hope. And when you do appear, may you find us living our lives in the way you have taught, waiting with an eager prayer on our lips, bearing the evidence of fruitful service in our lives and ready to welcome you with burning love and expectant faith.

I cannot tell how He will win the nations,
How He will claim His earthly heritage,
How satisfy the needs and aspirations
Of East and West, of sinner and of sage,
But this I know, all flesh shall see His glory,
And He shall reap the harvest He has sown,
And some glad day His sun shall shine in splendour
When He, the Saviour, Saviour of the world is known.

I cannot tell how all the lands shall worship,
When at His bidding, every storm is stilled,
Or who can say how great the jubilation
When all the hearts of men with love are filled.
But this I know, the skies will thrill with rapture
And myriad, myriad human voices sing,
And earth to heaven, and heaven to earth will answer:
At last the Saviour, Saviour of the world, is King!

William Young Fullerton

Even so, come, Lord Jesus!
Revelation 22:20

Waiting for the day

For centuries, Christians have tried to predict the precise date on which Jesus will return. As the year 1,000 approached, the level of excitement rose. Surely the Lord would choose to return in this year? But he did not come. In the twelfth century, a certain monk estimated that the world would end between 1200 and 1260. It did not. In more recent times, Jehovah's Witnesses speculated that the world as we know it would cease to exist in 1975. It did not. Neither had the present age closed in 1874, 1914, or 1915 as had been anticipated.

Christians who spend hours calculating the date of the Second Coming of Christ are not only wasting time, they are missing the point of Jesus' clear teaching. Jesus claimed complete ignorance of the date of his return:

> 'About that actual day and time no one knows – not even the angels in Heaven, nor the Son, only the Father. For just as life went on in the days of Noah so will it be at the coming of the Son of Man. In those days before the flood people were eating, drinking, marrying and being given in marriage until the very day that Noah went into the ark, and knew nothing about the flood until it came and destroyed them all. So it will be at the coming of the Son of Man. Two men will be in the field; one is taken and one is left behind. Two women will be grinding at the handmill; one is taken and one is left behind. You must be on the alert, then, for you do not know when your master is coming. You can be sure of this, however, that if the householder had known what time of night the burglar would arrive, he would have been ready for him and would not have allowed his house to be broken into. That is why you must always be ready, for you do not know what time the Son of Man will arrive.'
>
> Matthew 24:36-44

When Jesus returns, he will look for those who, though busy and active, are waiting for him with eagerness and trusting in him for their salvation. In such people he will expect to find behaviour which is worthy of those chosen to be representatives of his kingdom: those who are kind, patient, tolerant, forgiving and truly loving. As Paul wrote to the Colossians they should be those who 'have nothing to do with sexual immorality, dirty-mindedness, uncontrolled passion, evil desire, and the lust for other people's goods'.

'We must learn to behave in the presence of the invisible Lord as we would in the presence of the Lord made visible to us. This implies primarily an attitude of mind and then its reflection upon the body. If Christ was here, before us, and we stood completely transparent to his gaze, in mind as well as in body, we would feel reverence, the fear of God, adoration or else perhaps terror but *we should not be so easy in our behaviour as we are.'*

Archbishop Anthony Bloom

A glimpse of glory

We know that the precise date of Jesus' Second Coming is known only to the Father. But we are given a glimpse of what he will be like. We know, for example, that when he comes, he will come as a reigning, conquering King. John, the author of the Book of Revelation, helps us to picture the glory, the splendour and the majesty of the crowned King Jesus:

> 'I saw... what looked like a human being, wearing a robe that reached to his feet, and a gold belt round his chest. His hair was white as wool, or as snow, and his eyes blazed like fire; His feet shone like brass that had been refined and polished, and his voice sounded like a roaring waterfall. He held seven stars in his right hand, and a sharp two-edged sword came out of his mouth. His face was as bright as the midday sun. When I saw him, I fell down at his feet like a dead man. He placed his right hand on me and said: "Don't be afraid! I am the first and the last. I am the living one! I was dead, but now I am alive for ever and ever. I have authority over death and the world of the dead.'
>
> Revelation 1:9-18

The good news of Advent is that, when Jesus returns, we, too, shall see him, dressed in his kingly garments. We shall see him in all his purity and holiness. We shall see and hear and feel the immensity of his strength. And we shall be transfixed by his beauty.

> Alleluia, Alleluia!
> We are waiting for our Saviour,
> The Lord Jesus Christ,
> He will transfigure our lowly bodies
> Into copies of his own body
> Alleluia!
>
> The Weekday Missal

Lord Jesus, sometimes when I see a
spectacular sunset or witness the wonder of
the sunrise, I sense I catch a glimpse of your
glory. And sometimes, when the sight of a
snow-capped mountain causes me to catch my
breath, it reminds me of your greatness. But
this vision which you gave to John sets my
pulse racing and fills me with longing love and
the desire to be in your presence. Thank you
that you love me enough to come back to take
me into your glorious presence where I shall be
stunned with the wonder of who you are and
with your beauty.

O Lord my God, when I in awesome wonder
Consider all the works Thy hand hath made,
I see the stars, I hear the mighty thunder,
Thy pow'r throughout the universe displayed:

Then sings my soul, my Saviour, God, to Thee;
How great Thou art! How great Thou art!

When through the woods and forest glades I wander,
And hear the birds sing sweetly in the trees;
When I look down from lofty mountain grandeur,
And hear the brook, and feel the gentle breeze;

Then sings my soul, my Saviour, God, to Thee;
How great Thou art! How great Thou art!

When Christ shall come, with shouts of acclamation
And take me home – what joy shall fill my heart!
Then I shall bow in humble adoration,
And there proclaim, my God, how great Thou art!

Then sings my soul, my Saviour, God, to Thee;
How great Thou art! How great Thou art!
Stuart K. Hine

Ready and waiting

A friend of mine is moving house today. While she packs her belongings in boxes, I shall be looking after her baby. But I don't know quite when she will need me. When the baby wakes up she will telephone and ask me to come. I am ready to go at a moment's notice while trying to use my time sensibly and well, and not to waste it.

Although we do not know the date of Jesus' return, we do know how he wants us to behave during the waiting period:

> 'You must always be ready, for you do not
> know what time the Son of Man will arrive.'
> Matthew 24:44

Other passages of Scripture emphasize this same message:

> 'Be on your guard – see to it that your minds
> are never clouded by dissipation or
> drunkenness or the worries of this life, or else
> that day may catch you like the springing of a
> trap – for it will come upon every inhabitant of
> the whole earth.'
> Luke 21:34,35

> 'In those days the kingdom of Heaven will be
> like ten bridesmaids who took their lamps and
> went out to meet the bridegroom. Five of them
> were sensible and five were foolish. The
> foolish ones took their lamps but did not take
> any oil with them. But the sensible ones
> brought their lamps and oil in their flasks as
> well. Then, as the bridegroom was a very long
> time, they all grew drowsy and fell asleep. But
> in the middle of the night there came a shout,
> "Wake up, here comes the bridegroom! Out
> you go to meet him!" Then up got all the
> bridesmaids and attended to their lamps. The
> foolish ones said to the sensible ones, "Please
> give us some of your oil – our lamps are going
> out!" "Oh, no," returned the sensible ones,
> "there might not be enough for all of us. Better
> go to the oil-shop and buy some for
> yourselves." But while they had gone off to

buy the oil the bridegroom arrived, and those
bridesmaids who were ready went in with him
for the festivities and the door was shut
behind them. Later on the rest of the
bridesmaids came and said, "Oh, please, sir,
open the door for us!" But he replied, "I tell
you I don't know you!" So be on the alert – for
you do not know the day or the time.'

Matthew 25:1-13

In Israel, in the time of Jesus, the formalities of a marriage took place in three stages. First there was the engagement when a formal arrangement was made between the respective fathers of the bride and bridegroom. This was followed by the betrothal, a ceremony held in the home of the bride's parents during which promises were exchanged which committed the bride and groom to one another. About a year later, the marriage ceremony took place. The bridegroom would go to the bride's house, accompanied by his friends, who would walk in procession with the bride and groom back to the bridegroom's home.

In the story Jesus has the marriage ceremony in mind. He is the bridegroom and the bridesmaids represent Christians waiting for his return. The marriage feast symbolizes his second coming. And the message is both solemn and clear: Jesus' disciples must make sure that they are ready for his return. Those who fail to so prepare themselves will discover that the day of opportunity will have passed for ever. The wise bridesmaids live in a state of readiness. But the foolish ones refuse to face the possibility that the bridegroom might arrive earlier than they anticipated. They didn't have time to put things right. The wise bridesmaids, who are prepared, stress the simple truth that readiness is a personal possession. It cannot be transferred from one person to another.

Lord Jesus, in this 'waiting' time help me to live every day to the full and yet to live every day as though it were my last, so that, whenever you come, I may be ready to greet you with gladness, joy and welcoming love.

A time for action

'The hope of Christ's return is not a dogma to tickle our brains, but a fact to change our lives. Whenever the Bible speaks about Christ's second coming its purpose is always to challenge us to action... We are living "between the times" – between the time when Jesus introduced God's new era and the time when he will return to establish God's kingdom in its final form. Waiting for that momentous event is not a matter of sitting in our back gardens with our telescopes scanning the horizon. It is not a matter of killing time like waiting for a late train. It is a time for action, a time for distinctive Christian living.'

Stephen Travis

'Why all this stress on behaviour? Because, as I think you have realised, the present time is of the highest importance — it is time to wake up to reality. Every day brings God's salvation nearer.
The night is nearly over, the day has almost dawned. Let us therefore fling away the things that men do in the dark, let us arm ourselves for the fight of the day! Let us live cleanly, as in the daylight, not in the "delights" of getting drunk or playing with sex, nor yet in quarrelling or jealousies. Let us be Christ's men from head to foot, and give no chances to the flesh to have its fling.'

Romans 13:11-14

An attitude of readiness implies an attitude of repentance. Repentance means admitting where we have been failing or making mistakes, changing our mind about such behaviour, and turning around, to live life differently and in a disciplined manner. It involves telling God that we are sorry, receiving his forgiveness and asking for a fresh touch of his Spirit so that we are equipped for a life of obedience.

O Lord
My years grow long
And my time short
Let me make haste with my repentance
And bow both my head and heart
Let me not stay one day from amendment
Lest I stay too long
Let me cease without delay
To love my own mischief
And to abandon, without a backward look
The unfruitful works of darkness.
Lord, grant me new watchfulness
To lay hold upon opportunity for good
Make me at last put on the whole armour of light
Rank me among them who work for their Lord
Loins girded, lamps burning
Till the night shall pass
And the true light shine
Let me sing the new song
Following the lamb whithersoever he goes
Loving wheresoever he loves
Doing whatsoever he biddeth
Until the perfect day
The day of the true Advent
When the light comes into the world
For ever and ever.
Dean Milner-White

Servants of God

The Christians in the first century clearly took Jesus' teaching about his Second Coming seriously and literally. Some of them had been present at Jesus' Ascension. They had heard the two men dressed in white warn them:

> 'This very Jesus who has been taken up from you into Heaven will come back in just the same way as you have seen him go.'
>
> Acts 1:11

They took these words at face value and waited for Jesus to come back. In his Parable of the Talents, recorded in Matthew's Gospel, Chapter 25, Jesus shows us that this waiting is to be punctuated by a faithful, diligent use of all our gifts and talents. It is a story with a strong message: 'You must be on the alert... for you do not know when your master is coming...' And it shows how the three servants, each given different measures of responsibility by the master, use – or fail to use – what he has given them.

The master in this story is Jesus. The servants represent Christians. The sums of money signify the talents and possessions and knowledge of himself with which God has entrusted us.

What Jesus is implying here is that his chosen people not only enjoy certain privileges, but they must also accept certain responsibilities. As we wait eagerly for Jesus to return, our responsibility is to invest our possessions and talents in the service of God and other people, and to obey God's instructions. Such investment will be rewarded. But if, when the accounts are settled, we are found to have squandered these treasures, we, too, shall weep and wail over our slothfulness and the choices we have made.

Heavenly Father, thank you for the talents you have given me, especially for the gift of
....
and ....
Thank you, too, for the possessions you have entrusted me with: my home, my money, my books, my time. May I take seriously this parable of Jesus and re-dedicate each of these things to you. Show me how I can best use them to bring others into your Kingdom or to alleviate pain and suffering. May I live, always, in a way which brings you pleasure.

No more pain

Life on earth is an inevitable mix of joy and pain. Indeed, life is full of disappointments and frustrations. Sometimes the pain of personal failure, the loss of loved ones or the fear of the future feels almost intolerable. It is then that the message of Advent, with the hope that it brings in its wake, is most comforting, even healing. For Advent reminds us that when Jesus returns, life will be very different. John gives us a glimpse of life lived in the eternal presence of the returning Christ:

> 'Then I saw a new Heaven and a new earth, for the first Heaven and the first earth had disappeared and the sea was no more. I saw the Holy City, the New Jerusalem, descending from God out of Heaven, prepared as a Bride dressed in beauty for her husband. Then I heard a great voice from the throne crying,
> "See! The home of God is with men, and he will live among them. They shall be his people, and God himself shall be with them, and will wipe away every tear from their eyes. Death shall be no more, and never again shall there be sorrow or crying or pain. For all those former things are past and gone." '
>
> Revelation 21:1-4

When we have experienced what the Psalmist once described as 'tears have been my meat day and night', the thought of a time and place where tears and loss and sorrow and sighing cease for ever seems almost too good to be true. But John assures us of the awesome fact that when Jesus returns, this will be our experience.

Isaiah, too, reminds us of the tenderness of God which will bring such joy when Jesus returns to claim us for his own:

> 'He will feed his flock like a shepherd,
> he will gather the lambs in his arms,
> he will carry them in his bosom,
> and gently lead those that are with young.'
>
> Isaiah 40:11

Lord Jesus,
Thank you that you love me,
not in some aloof, impersonal way,
but with the cherishing love a mother pours on her child;
with the protective love with which a shepherd
shields his vulnerable lamb
and with the cherishing love a good father delights
to give to his first-born.
Thank you that your love for me now
is a long-suffering love.
Faithful
devoted
unchanging
inextinguishable.
And thank you
that on that glorious day when I see you face to face
I shall experience that love
in rich measure;
I shall live eclipsed by that love
for all eternity.

No more striving

I once read a story by Trina Paulus about a caterpillar whose name was **Yellow**. She used to dream of becoming a butterfly but doubted that this liberating thing could ever happen to her: *'How can I believe there's a butterfly inside me when all I see is a fuzzy worm?'*

One day, Yellow met a fellow caterpillar who encouraged her to believe that she could be transformed. She decided to take the risk: to lose the life she knew, the caterpillar state, and to weave around herself the cocoon from which she would emerge as a butterfly. Her friends waited.

Their patience was rewarded. Rising before their eyes was a brilliant, yellow, winged creature: it was the same **Yellow** they had always known and yet so very different. She looked awesome as she soared into the sky, circled round and gloried in the air she had now inherited. Her freedom was enchanting.

The apostle Paul, writing in Romans, reminds us that, while this life lasts, we, too, are rather like caterpillars, 'groaning inwardly while we wait for God to... set our whole body free.' Paul also encourages us to believe that when Jesus returns, we shall no longer need to strive to be like him; the transformation will be instant and complete:

> 'Listen! I will unfold a mystery: we shall not all die, but we shall all be changed in a flash, in the twinkling of an eye, at the last trumpet-call. For the trumpet will sound, and the dead will rise immortal, and we shall be changed. This perishable being must be clothed with the imperishable, and what is mortal must be clothed with immortality. And when our mortality has been clothed with immortality, then the saying of Scripture will come true: "Death is swallowed up; victory is won!" "O Death, where is your victory? O Death, where is your sting?"... God be praised, he gives us the victory through our Lord Jesus Christ.'
>
> I Corinthians 15:51-57

In other words, when Jesus returns, we shall be free at last: free from death, and free from struggling and striving; free to be what God wants us to be.

Come, Thou long-expected Jesus,
Born to set Thy people free;
From our fears and sins release us;
Let us find our rest in Thee.

Born Thy people to deliver,
Born a child and yet a king.
Born to reign in us for ever,
Now Thy gracious kingdom bring.

By Thine own eternal Spirit
Rule in all our hearts alone;
By Thine all-sufficient merit
Raise us to Thy glorious throne.

Charles Wesley

No more sin

As I write these meditations, seventy people are being held hostage in a hijacked aeroplane and two of these have just been shot. A few days ago, a taxi driver was murdered while driving a miner to work. More trouble is brewing in the Middle East. Terrorism and vandalism are on the increase. The number of rape cases is causing alarm. Elderly people and women are frightened to go out alone at night. Meanwhile, the number of muggings in the home is escalating. And news reaches us regularly of thousands of people dying every day in famine-stricken Africa while people in the West live in luxury. But when Jesus returns to take us to be with himself, all that will change. St John writes:

> 'Then I saw a new heaven and a new earth, for the first heaven and the first earth had passed away... I saw the Holy City... I did not see a temple in the city, because the Lord God Almighty and the Lamb are its temple. The city does not need the sun or the moon to shine on it, for the glory of God gives it light, and the Lamb is its lamp. The nations will walk by its light, and the kings of the earth will bring their splendour into it. On no day will its gates ever be shut, for there will be no night there... Nothing impure will ever enter it, nor will anyone who does what is shameful or deceitful, but only those whose names are written in the Lamb's book of life.'
>
> Revelation 21:1,22-27

The Lamb whose brightness lights the city is none other than Jesus himself. John records Jesus' own promise that his kingdom will be free from any sort of pollution. Pure. Sinless.

> 'Blessed are those who wash their robes, that they may have the right to the tree of life and may go through the gates into the city. Outside are the dogs, those who practise magic arts, the sexually immoral, the murderers, the idolators and everyone who loves and practises falsehood.'
>
> Revelation 22:14-15

The message of Advent is clear: the purity of God and the filthiness of sin cannot co-exist. In the new Jerusalem security

28

measures will no longer be necessary because evil will no longer exist.

The challenge of Advent is this: if we would live in that sinless place, heaven, we must make every effort to deal with the sin we detect in our own lives and which plagues us now. As St Augustine reminds us: 'The last day is hidden that every day may be regarded.'

> At the name of Jesus
> Every knee shall bow,
> Every tongue confess Him
> King of glory now;
> 'Tis the Father's pleasure
> We should call Him Lord,
> Who from the beginning
> Was the mighty Word.
>
> Humbled for a season
> To receive a name
> From the lips of sinners,
> Unto whom He came;
> Faithfully He bore it
> Spotless to the last;
> Brought it back victorious
> When from death He passed.
>
> In your hearts enthrone Him;
> There let Him subdue
> All that is not holy,
> All that is not true:
> Crown Him as your Captain
> In temptation's hour;
> Let His will enfold you
> In its light and power.
>
> Brothers, this Lord Jesus
> Shall return again,
> With His Father's glory,
> With His angel train;
> For all wreaths of empire
> Meet upon His brow
> And our hearts confess Him
> King of glory now.
> Caroline Maria Noel

Eternal Light, shine into our hearts,
Eternal Goodness, deliver us from evil,
Eternal Power, be our support,
Eternal Wisdom, scatter the darkness of our ignorance,

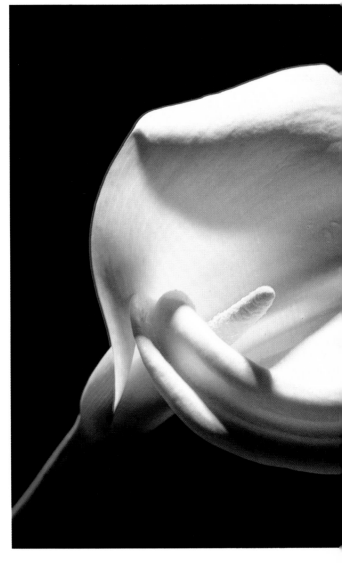

Eternal Pity, have mercy upon us;
that with all our heart and mind and soul and strength
we may seek thy face and be brought by thine infinite mercy
to thy holy presence; through Jesus Christ our Lord.
Alcuin of York

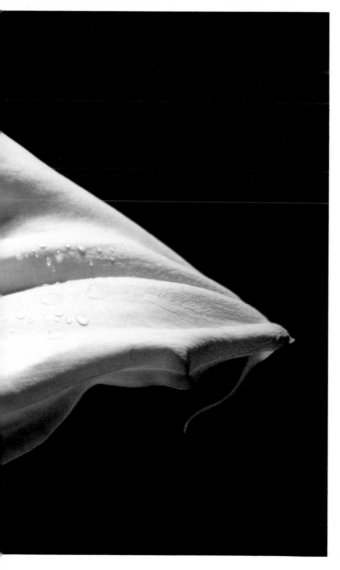

Jesus the Judge

On the first Christmas Day, Jesus arrived into the world of ordinary, everyday life, unannounced, unwanted and unexpected. When he comes back, his arrival will be similarly unexpected. But this time he will not come as a helpless, dependent baby. This time he will come as the Judge of the entire world. Many Christians today find this an uncomfortable truth; one which they would prefer to ignore.

'We live, in this twentieth century, in a world without judgement, a world where at the last frontier post you simply go out – nothing happens. It is like coming to the customs and finding there are none after all. And the suspicion that this is in fact the case spreads fast: for it is what we should all like to believe.'

John Robinson

But the Gospel writers give us no licence to accept such beliefs. On the contrary, they show that judgment is inescapable, serious, just and that in one sense, it has already begun. Our attitude to God today, the choices we make today, the lifestyle we decide on today, determine our destiny. Judgment is not like finals: you pass or fail on the strength of one set of exams. Judgment is more like continuous assessment. That is why, in Advent, Christians prepare themselves, not just for Christmas, but for eternity, by weighing some of the admonitions of Jesus. Matthew's Gospel shows what will happen when Jesus returns as king.

The nations will gather at his feet and Jesus will invite some people to 'possess the kingdom' because:

' "I was hungry and you fed me, thirsty and you gave me drink; I was a stranger and you received me in your homes, naked and you clothed me; I was sick and you took care of me, in prison and you visited me."
'The righteous will then answer him, "When, Lord, did we ever see you hungry and feed you, or thirsty and give you drink? When did we ever see you a stranger and welcome you in our homes or naked and clothe you? When did we ever see you sick or in prison, and visit you?" The King will reply, "I tell you, whenever you did this for one of the least important of these brothers of mine, you did it for me!" '
To those who have refused to help 'one of these least important ones', he says: ' "Away from me, you that are under God's curse! Away to the eternal fire which has been prepared for the Devil and his angels! ...These, then, will be sent to eternal punishment, but the righteous will go to eternal life." '

Matthew 25:35-40; 41,46

Lord Jesus, thank you for this rebuke which goads me out of my false complacency. Forgive me that, while I try to decide what to have for supper, I forget that one quarter of your world suffers from poverty. Forgive me that when, on impulse, I go to buy new clothes which I do not need, I ignore the fact that thirty million children will die of starvation this year. You have pricked my conscience. Now goad me into action. Govern my attitudes, and become the Lord of my lifestyle. May the choices I make be considered rather than impetuous. May those I meet be touched by the overflowing of your love. And may all that I do bring pleasure to your watching eyes now, in this life, so that I may enjoy your presence for all eternity.

The downfall of Satan

As we look forward to the new heaven and new earth, we look forward to the time when Satan – God's enemy – will be completely and utterly vanquished.

The Bible encourages us to believe in 'a Satan, and a host of Satanic myrmidons, who are of quite unimaginable badness – more cruel, more malicious, more proud, more scornful, more perverted, more destructive, more disgusting, more filthy, more despicable, than anything our minds can conceive,' as Jim Packer describes him.

Peter in his letter also shows us that this evil is the enemy of our souls:

> 'Your enemy the devil prowls around like a roaring lion looking for someone to devour.'
> 1 Peter 5:8

Paul makes it clear that we must be on our guard against this professional liar whose power is immense and efficiently executed:

> 'For our fight is not against human foes, but against cosmic powers, against the authorities and potentates of this dark world, against the superhuman forces of evil in the heavens.'
> Ephesians 6:12

At the moment, Satan does counterfeit miracles, implants impure thoughts in our minds, dresses temptation up to make it look attractive, inflicts diseases on people and holds them in spiritual bondage.

But when Jesus comes, all this will change. When Jesus finally takes his power and reigns, we shall witness Satan's downfall. This was the reason why Jesus came to earth in the first place:

> 'The reason the Son of God appeared was to destroy the devil's work.'
> 1 John 3:8

But, as Michael Green explains, when Jesus died on the cross he inflicted a mortal wound on Satan, robbing the world of evil of its power:

'Christ is the conqueror over all the power of the Enemy, and on the cross he inflicted such a crushing defeat on the devil that whenever his name is named in faith, Satan is bound to flee.'

Even so, Satan is allowed some rein. But John foresees the day when this dramatic conquest of good over evil will be complete:

> 'Then I saw an angel coming down from Heaven with the key of the pit and a huge chain in his hand. He seized... Satan, and bound him fast... Then he hurled him into the pit, and locked and sealed it over his head, so that he could deceive the nations no more... The devil... was hurled into the lake of fire and sulphur... And there (he) shall be tortured day and night for timeless ages.'
>
> Revelation 20:1-3; 10

> Jesus! The name high over all,
> In hell, or earth, or sky;
> Angels and men before it fall,
> And devils fear and fly.
>
> Jesus the prisoner's fetters breaks
> And bruises Satan's head;
> Power into strengthless souls it speaks,
> And life into the dead.
>
> Happy, if with my latest breath
> I might but gasp His name;
> Preach Him to all, and cry in death:
> Behold, behold the Lamb!
>
> Charles Wesley

The grand reunion

When someone we love dies, we feel keenly their absence. The sense of loss and loneliness can hold us in its grip for many months. At such times, the thought of the grand reunion we shall enjoy when Jesus returns can bring untold comfort:

'Now we don't want you, my brothers, to be in any doubt about those who "fall asleep" in death, or to grieve over them like men who have no hope. After all, if we believe that Jesus died and rose again from death, then we can believe that God will just as surely bring with Jesus all who are "asleep" in him... Those who have died in Christ will be the first to rise... And after that we shall be with him for ever.'

1 Thessalonians 4:13-15; 17

'The principal happiness of heaven is this, *to be with the Lord,* to see him, live with him, and enjoy him, for ever. This should comfort (Christians) upon the death of their friends. We and they... shall meet our Lord, and be with him for ever, no more to be separated either from him or from one another for ever.'

Matthew Henry

Lord Jesus Christ,
Sometimes, I close my eyes and try to imagine
what it will be like
When you come in glory.
Will the sky blush, as with the sunrise?
Or will it glow as it does when the sun sets?
Or will your glory pierce through the clouds in
a sudden blaze of light?
Who can tell?
And who can tell how that grand reunion with
loved ones will happen?
Amid all these imponderables, thank you for
the certainty
That when you come to take us home
Our loved ones who loved you while they were
here on earth will be with you
And we shall be with you
In that place where death has lost its sting
Where goodbyes become a thing of the past
Where there is no more parting
Either from those we love
Or from you.

For ever with the Lord

At the end of John Bunyan's book *Pilgrim's Progress,* the hero of the story, Christian, comes at last to the river over which he must cross before he enters the Holy City: Heaven. Ministering spirits come to him to encourage him as he embarks on the last lap of the journey. They describe to him what life will be like when he reaches the other side:

' "There," said they, "is the Mount Sion, the heavenly Jerusalem, the innumerable company of angels, and the spirits of just men made perfect; you are going now... to the Paradise of God... and when you come there you shall have white robes given you, and your walk and talk shall be every day with the King, even all the days of eternity. There you shall not see again such things as you saw when you were in the lower region upon the earth... sorrow, sickness, affliction and death, *for the former things are passed away.*
' "...Then I heard in my dream, that all the bells in the City rang again for joy; and that it was said unto them *"Enter into the joy of your Lord."* I also heard the men themselves, that they sang with a loud voice, saying, *"Blessing, honour, glory, and power be to him that sitteth upon the throne, and to the Lamb for ever and ever." '*
John Bunyan

The apostle John gives us another glimpse of the joy that will be ours when Jesus comes to claim us for himself:

'I looked again, and before my eyes appeared a vast crowd beyond man's power to number. They came from every nation and tribe and people and language, and they stood before the throne of the Lamb, dressed in white robes with palm-branches in their hands... Then all the angels stood encircling the throne, the elders and the four living creatures, and prostrated themselves with heads bowed before the throne and worshipped God, saying, "Amen! Blessing and glory and wisdom and thanksgiving and honour and power and strength be given to our God for timeless ages!"... And then I heard a sound like the voices of a vast crowd, the roar of a great waterfall and the rolling of heavy thunder, and they were saying, "Alleluia! For the Lord our God, the Almighty, has come into his kingdom! Let us rejoice, let us be glad with all our hearts. Let us give him the glory, for the wedding-day of the Lamb has come, and his bride has made herself ready. She may be seen dressed in linen, gleaming and spotless – for such linen is the righteous living of the saints!"

Revelation 7:9-12

At your feet we fall, mighty risen Lord
As we come before your throne to worship you,
By your Spirit's power you now draw our hearts,
And we hear your voice in triumph ringing clear.
I am he that liveth, that liveth and was dead,
Behold I am alive for evermore.

Through nature

When Yuri Gagarin, the first man in space, returned to earth, he is reported to have said that he had not seen God on his travels. A Russian priest, on hearing this observation, commented: 'If you haven't seen God on earth, you will never see him in heaven.'

But how do we find God on earth? This is a heart-felt question many people voice. One man put it this way: 'I have been trying for years to work on the pattern of prayer laid down in devotional books but what I really want to know is how to pray my life, not how to use fifteen minutes out of my life.'

The Bible shows us how we may see God on earth and how we may learn to pray continually. One thing it exhorts us to do is to walk around with our eyes open and to contemplate nature, for in doing so we see various expressions of God in the things that he has created.

'The heavens declare the glory of God;
the skies proclaim the work of his hands.'

Psalm 19:1

God –
spread out the earth upon the waters...
made the great lights...
the sun to govern the day...
the moon and stars to govern the night...
Give thanks to the God of heaven.'

from Psalm 136

'Look at the birds flying around: they do not sow seeds,
gather a harvest and put it in barns; your Father in
heaven takes care of them!'

Matthew 6:26

'Nature never taught me that there exists a God of glory and of infinite majesty. I had to learn that in other ways. But nature gave the word glory meaning for me. I still do not know where else I could have found one.'

C.S. Lewis

Turn my gaze, dear Lord, that I may see you in the world around me as I prepare for the birthday of your son.

Real joy in everyday life

The days leading up to Christmas are, for many of us, the most hectic of the year. So much has to be pushed into so few hours, it seems. For the Christian who longs to focus on the true meaning of Christmas – the fact that at this time of year we remember that God sent his Son into the world to be our Saviour – this busyness poses a problem. How can we enjoy to the full the special joys of Christmas-time: the fun, the festivities and the family togetherness, and yet remain God-centred?

Jesus gives us one clue when he reminds us that, through the Holy Spirit, he and the Father will come to take up residence in us:

> 'If anyone loves me, he will obey my teaching. My Father will love him, and we will come to him and make our home with him.'
>
> John 14:23

Paul gives us two more clues:

> 'Whatever you do, work at it with all your heart, as working for the Lord, not for men.'
>
> Colossians 3:23

> 'Pray continually'
>
> 1 Thessalonians 5:17

This praying is not so much the saying of words as the awareness of a presence.

Brother Lawrence, the cook in a busy thirteenth-century monastery, testifies that he was as conscious of God's presence when elbow-deep in potato peelings as he was when worshipping God in chapel. And it is said of St Teresa of Avila that she found God so easily among the pots and pans that she rejoiced in an acute awareness of the God who was her constant companion even in the middle of the chaos.

The God who came to this monk and this nun, still comes if we have eyes to see him and ears to hear him.

42

Lord Jesus
What these men and women achieved –
The awareness of your over-shadowing
And your in-dwelling –
I covet.
Give me, dear Lord,
The consciousness, as I work,
Of your presence in the room.
The awareness, as I drive,
Of a beloved passenger by my side.
The assurance even in the maelstrom of the
supermarket or my place of work
Of the love of the Lord
Who holds together the many strands that
intertwine
To make up my life
To make of them one strong, resilient whole.

Teach me, my God and King,
In all things Thee to see,
And what I do in anything
To do it as for Thee!

George Herbert

In the day's pauses

No matter how busy we are, no matter how full our days, we all pause from time to time. We take a coffee break, a lunch break, a tea break. The busy typist pauses to remove paper from the typewriter, the teacher walks from one classroom to another, the hairdresser waits while the curling tongs warm up, the doctor drives to the surgery.

We can train ourselves to use these pauses, not simply to acknowledge that Jesus is with us, but to go further and use them to shoot up 'arrow' prayers to God.

It seems that this method of prayer came to Jesus quite naturally. One day, in the middle of talking to his disciples, he suddenly broke off the conversation and started to talk aloud to his Father:

> 'I praise you, Father, Lord of heaven and earth, because you have hidden these things from the wise and learned, and revealed them to little children.'
> Matthew 11:25

Similarly, just before he miraculously fed five thousand people:

> 'He took the five loaves and two fish, looked up to heaven, and gave thanks to God.'
> Matthew 14:19

In this way, even surrounded by people in need, Jesus kept in close touch with his Father. It is not difficult for us to do the same; to find God coming to us in the middle of our activities as we turn our hearts and minds towards him.

We find many such prayers recorded in the Bible. These can become a part of our vocabulary of prayer:

> 'Lord, save us. We're going to drown!'
> Jesus' disciples in a storm on the Sea of Galilee

> 'Praise the Lord, O my soul and all that is within me praise his holy name.'
> Psalm 103:1

When faced with a choice:

> 'Your will, not mine, be done.'
> Jesus, in the Garden of Gethsemane

In times of temptation:

> 'Away from me, Satan'
> Jesus, in Matthew 4:10

When we call out these short prayers to our Father in heaven, we are so lifted above earthly things that we become conscious of being upheld by God. And when we school ourselves to pray like this on and off during the day, our special times of quiet take on a new significance. Because the mind and the heart have not been allowed to wander too far from God, when we are able to come before him in prolonged stillness, we relax in him with ease, tune into his presence with gratitude and are guided by him afresh as we learn to seek his will and his way in the practicalities of life.

O Sabbath rest by Galilee!
O calm of hills above,
Where Jesus knelt to share with thee
The silence of eternity,
Interpreted by love!

Drop thy still dews of quietness,
Till all our strivings cease;
Take from our souls the strain and stress,
And let our ordered lives confess
The beauty of thy peace.

Breathe through the heats of our desire
Thy coolness and thy balm;
Let sense be dumb, let flesh retire;
Speak through the earthquake, wind, and fire,
O still small voice of calm!

John Greenleaf Whittier

Oh, come to us, abide with us,
Our Lord Emmanuel.

In the stillness

God comes to us through nature. God comes to us in our busyness. God comes to us through things and through people. But God comes to us most powerfully in moments when we are silent before him.

When Jesus was busiest, he made time to be still before his Father. Similarly, God commands us to be silent:

'Be still, and know that I am God.'
Psalm 46:10

Even at this busy time of year, if we are going to be still like this, we need a time and a place where we can meet with God on our own.

'There should be at least a room, or some corner where no one will find you and disturb you or notice you. You should be able to untether yourself from the world and set yourself free, loosing all the fine strings and strands of tension that bind you, by sight, by sound, by thought, to the presence of other men.

'Once you have found such a place, be content with it... Love it, and return to it as soon as you can, and do not be too quick to change it for another.'
Thomas Merton

Seek silence: it brings us near to God.
In silence: God's still, small voice is heard.
Out of silence: true peace is born in our hearts.

> *The Lord is my Pace-setter, I shall not rush.*
> *He makes me stop and rest for quiet intervals.*
> *He provides me with images of stillness*
> *Which restore my serenity.*
> *He leads me in ways of efficiency through*
> *calmness of mind, and His guidance is peace.*
> *Even though I have a great many things to*
> *accomplish each day*
> *I will not fret*
> *For His presence is there.*
> *His timelessness, His all-importance,*
> *Will keep me in balance.*
> *He prepares refreshment and renewal*
> *In the midst of my activity.*
> *By anointing my mind with His oils of*
> *tranquillity*
> *My cup of joyous energy overflows.*
> *Surely harmony and effectiveness*
> *Shall be the fruits of my hours,*
> *For I shall walk in the pace of my Lord,*
> *And dwell in His house for ever.*
> Toki Miyashina

> *Still my heart, O God, that I may be ready*
> *to worship you this Christmas.*

Through ordinary things of life

God comes to us through ordinary things. In his teaching, Jesus so often referred to the ordinary, everyday things of life, showing how they point to God at work in our world. Speaking to a culture where it was the custom for women to wear their wealth in the form of bands of silver coins around the forehead, he used an everyday example to show us an aspect of God's character:

> 'Suppose a woman has ten silver coins and loses one. Does she not light a lamp, sweep the house and search carefully until she finds it? And when she finds it, she calls her friends and neighbours together and says, "Rejoice with me; I have found my lost coin." In the same way, I tell you, there is rejoicing in the presence of the angels of God over one sinner who repents.'
> Luke 15:8-10

Again, he uses an ordinary, everyday lamp to make another point about the kingdom:

> 'No-one lights a lamp and hides it in a jar or puts it under a bed. Instead, he puts it on a stand, so that those who come in can see the light. For there is nothing hidden that will not be disclosed, and nothing concealed that will not be known or brought out into the open. Therefore consider carefully how you listen.'
> Luke 8:16-17

He even used something as domesticated and seemingly insignificant as yeast to illustrate his teaching:

> 'The kingdom of heaven is like yeast that a woman took and mixed into a large amount of flour until it worked all through the dough.'
> Matthew 13:33

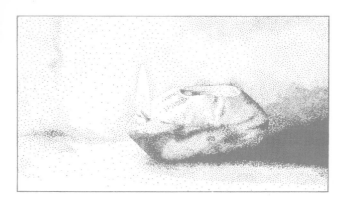

Clearly, Jesus was a man who walked round with his eyes open. He used everything his Father had created as an opportunity to encounter the Father afresh.

And if we are sincere in praying that God will come to us, we, too, can find him through mundane things.

'If we knew how to look at life through God's eyes, we should see it as innumerable tokens of the love of the Creator seeking the love of his creatures. The Father has put us into the world, not to walk through it with lowered eyes, but to search for him through things, events, people.
Everything must reveal God to us.
Long prayers are not needed in order to smile at Christ in the smallest details of daily life...
If we knew how to listen to God, if we knew how to look around us, our whole life would become prayer.'
Michel Quoist

*Even in the busyness of this time of year, dear Lord,
let me pause to smile at you: the babe of Bethlehem.*

Through love

'Love is like the hook on a fisherman's line; the fish must take the hook or the fisherman can never catch him. After the hook is once in his mouth, the fish may swim about and even swim away from the shore, but the fisherman is sure to finally land him. And this I compare with love. Whoever is caught by love is held perfectly fast, and yet in a sweet captivity. Whoever has received the gift of divine love... he it is that can most sweetly endure all misfortunes that happen to him or threaten to overwhelm him; he is the one who most readily forgives all the injuries that can be inflicted on him.'
John Tauler

'Dear friends! Let us love one another, for love comes from God. Whoever loves is a child of God and knows God. Whoever does not love does not know God, because God is love... We should love one another. No one has ever seen God; if we love one another, God lives in us and his love is made perfect within us... We love because God first loved us.'
1 John 4:7-8; 11; 19

Signs of the love of friends surround me as I look around my home. There is the little vase on the window-sill of my study given to me by a couple I love, the candle-holder made for me by a friend from an antique piece of yew, the books on my shelves, signed and sent as gifts by their authors, the photograph, framed and sent to me by the photographer one Christmas, the card I kept because it bears the inscription *'Thank you for our friendship'*.

God's love comes to us most powerfully through people. That is why Christmas can be so special: at this time of year we make a special effort to ensure that our friends know they are valued and loved by us.

Lord Jesus, thank you that so often you choose to come to me through the expressed love of friends: through the warmth of their embrace; through the unexpected telephone call; through the card arriving on the very day I needed encouragement. Sometimes, dear Lord, you seem a long way away. But I can hear the language of human touch, the human voice and the written message. May I learn more and more to drink in the fact that all this love comes from you; that perfect love is what you are; that you are the source of love and its fulfilment. For every expression of your love to me, I thank you. Make me more worthy to receive your love, no matter how it is expressed. And may I be so hooked by it that I, in turn, learn how to love - to love you and to allow you to love others through me.

Love divine, all loves excelling,
Joy of heaven to earth come down,
Fix in us Thy humble dwelling,
All Thy faithful mercies crown.

Jesus, Thou art all compassion,
Pure, unbounded love Thou art;
Visit us with Thy salvation,
Enter every longing heart.

Come, almighty to deliver,
Let us all Thy life receive;
Suddenly return, and never,
Never more Thy temples leave.

Charles Wesley

Through his Son

God comes to us in a whole variety of ways: through nature, through silence, through the love of friends. But the most amazing way so far, has been the coming of God's Son, the 'word made flesh'.

> God, who gave to our forefathers many different glimpses of the truth in the words of the prophets, has now, at the end of the present age, given us the truth in the Son. Through the Son God made the whole universe, and to the Son he has ordained that all creation shall ultimately belong. This Son, radiance of the glory of God, flawless expression of the nature of God, himself the upholding principle of all that is, effected in person the reconciliation between God and man and then took his seat at the right hand of the majesty on high.
>
> Hebrews 1:1-4

JESUS
radiance of the glory of God
flawless expression of the nature of God
creator of the universe

This is the one who came to earth as a tiny vulnerable baby! God showed us how much he loved us by allowing this essential part of himself to make his entry to earth and to live among us as one of us – as a man.

> 'This is how God showed his love among us: he sent his one and only Son into the world that we might live through him. This is love: not that we loved God, but that he loved us and sent his Son as an atoning sacrifice for our sins.'
>
> 1 John 4:9-11

'It is the simple fact that men did not know what God was like until Jesus came. The Greeks thought of a passionless God, beyond all joy and sorrow, looking on men in calm unmoved detachment – no help there. The Jews thought of a demanding God, whose name was law and whose function was that of Judge – nothing but terror there. Jesus came to tell of a God who was love, and in staggered amazement men could only

say, "We never knew that God was like that." One of the functions of the incarnation is to bring men the knowledge of God... The distant God is become near and the God we feared has become the lover of the souls of men.'

William Barclay

Heavenly Father,
As we await the birthday of your Son, Jesus Christ,
Give us a glimpse of the mystery of the incarnation.
Cause us to wonder that the Creator of the universe
Emptied himself of the splendour and glory of heaven
And took upon himself the feeble frame of a fragile baby.
Restore to us the ability to stop
The serenity to ponder
And the creativity to gaze in wonder
At the Christ-child –
The radiance of the glory of God –
The flawless expression of the divine nature
At God made man
God in human form
God manifesting himself with a vulnerability which asks
To be touched
And handled and seen and known and loved.
And teach us to love you without inhibition
That this Christmas the glow in our hearts
May bring joy to you, Father, Son and Holy Spirit.

God prepares for the birth of his Son

Just as Christmas is a busy time for us, so the first Christmas was a busy time for God. He knew that the Jews were not yet ready to receive the Saviour of the world. Their hearts were hardened. They were spiritually blind. Someone would have to herald the Messiah's arrival. Luke tells us who that someone was. He also reveals the series of miracles which led up to this person's birth.

The story, recorded in the first chapter of Luke, tells of the miraculous way God intervened in the lives of Elizabeth and Zechariah, an old priest and his wife. Childless for many years and faithful people of God, they were chosen by God to become the parents of John the Baptist.

Luke tells how Zechariah received a message from one of God's angels:

> '"Do not be afraid, Zechariah; your prayers have been heard. Elizabeth your wife will bear you a son, and you are to call him John. This will be joy and delight to you and many more will be glad because he is born. He will be one of God's great men; he will touch neither wine nor strong drink and he will be filled with the Holy Spirit from the moment of his birth. He will turn many of Israel's children to the Lord their God ... and he will make a people fully ready for their Lord."
>
> But Zechariah replied to the angel,
> "How can I know that this is true? I am an old man myself and my wife is getting on in years..."
> "I am Gabriel," the angel answered. "I stand in the presence of God, and I have been sent to speak to you and tell you this good news. Because you do not believe what I have said, you shall live in silence, and you shall be unable to speak a word until the day that it happens. But be sure that everything that I have told you will come true at the proper time...."
> He went back home, and soon afterwards his wife Elizabeth became pregnant and kept herself secluded for five months.

"How good the Lord is to me," she would say, "now that he has taken away the shame that I have suffered."'

Luke 1:13-20, 24-25

Zechariah was a priest. It was while he was going about his priestly duties that God met him in this astonishing way. Elizabeth was a housewife; one who longed to be a mother. It was while she suffered the anguish many childless women suffer that God met her in a miraculous way. And so often it is while we go about our everyday tasks – attending carol services, writing Christmas cards, buying presents – that God comes to us.

Father, thank you that the miracle you did for Zechariah and Elizabeth boosts my ability to believe in you. Thank you that the age of miracles is not past and that you still intervene in the lives of men and women today. This Christmas, dear Lord, I long to encounter you afresh. Whether I'm praying or busy doing all the things that have to be done, touch my heart and warm it. Remove from my eyes the scales of unbelief. Take from me the heart of stone that refuses to respond to you. Prepare me so that I am ready to receive you with awe and wonder, joy and thanksgiving and grateful love.

Thou didst leave Thy throne
And Thy kingly crown
When Thou camest to earth for me;
But in Bethlehem's home
Was there found no room
For Thy holy nativity:
Oh come to my heart, Lord Jesus;
There is room in my heart for Thee.

Emily E. Steele Elliott

The birth of Jesus is announced

The little town of Nazareth nestled on the slopes of the mountains of Lower Galilee. Its busy, narrow streets rose above the market place in terraces and its houses were small with flat roofs.

The countryside was fragrant with the scent of orange and lemon blossom and aromatic plants. The fields were bright with wild flowers: scarlet anemones, golden crown daisies, and bright-eyed marguerites. Gnarled fig trees, silvery olive trees, dark green cypress trees and graceful palm trees formed a familiar landscape.

In this town lived an ordinary young woman named Mary. We know little about her except that she was probably still in her teens and engaged to a carpenter named Joseph when the same angel who had appeared to Zechariah visited her:

'"Greetings to you, Mary, O favoured one! – the Lord be with you!"
Mary was deeply perturbed at these words and wondered what such a greeting could possibly mean.
But the angel said to her,
"Do not be afraid, Mary; God loves you dearly. You are going to be the mother of a son, and you will call him Jesus. He will be great and will be known as the Son of the most high. The Lord God will give him the throne of his forefather, David, and he will be king over the people of Jacob for ever. His reign shall never end."
Then Mary spoke to the angel,
"How can this be," she said, "I am not married!"
But the angel made this reply to her
"The Holy Spirit will come upon you, the power of the most high will overshadow you. Your child will therefore be called holy – the Son of God."
"...I belong to the Lord, body and soul," replied Mary, "Let it happen as you say." And at this the angel left her.'

Luke 1:26-38

56

Here we see the amazing fact of the Creator of the universe
seeking the co-operation of an ordinary young woman to
break into the history of the world which he himself created.
And we see Mary's beautiful act of submission. In this way,
Mary became the selfless space where God could become man.

> *Here I am*
> *Wholly available*
> *As for me*
> *I will serve the Lord*

Mary's song of praise

Every Jewish woman secretly hoped that she would be chosen to be the mother of the Messiah. To Mary this immense privilege was given. Like most of us, Mary needed to share her good news:

'With little delay Mary got ready and hurried off to the hill-side town in Judaea where Zechariah and Elizabeth lived. She went into their house and greeted her cousin. When Elizabeth heard her greeting, the unborn child stirred inside her and she herself was filled with the Holy Spirit, and cried out,
"Blessed are you among women, and blessed is your child! What an honour it is to have the mother of my Lord come to see me! Why, as soon as your greeting reached my ears, the child within me jumped for joy! Oh, how happy is the woman who believes in God, for he does make his promises to her come true."
Then Mary said, "My heart is overflowing with praise of my Lord, my soul is full of joy in God my Saviour. For he has deigned to notice me, his humble servant and, after this, all the people who ever shall be will call me the happiest of women! The one who can do all things has done great things for me – oh, holy is his Name! Truly, his mercy rests on those who fear him in every generation. He has shown the strength of his arm, he has swept away the high and mighty. He has set kings down from their thrones and lifted up the humble. He has satisfied the hungry with good things and sent the rich away with empty hands. Yes, he has helped Israel, his child: he has remembered the mercy that he promised to our forefathers, to Abraham and his sons for evermore!"'

Luke 1:39-55

One of the wonderful things was that Mary did not have to spell out her good news. God had already revealed it to Elizabeth. Any doubts or fears that Mary may have had must have been dispelled as God used Elizabeth's welcome to confirm the truth to her. The other wonderful thing was that the two women could rejoice together in the pure goodness of God.

In her song of praise, Mary worships God from the depths of her being. Despite her poverty and obscurity, God had chosen her to be the mother of the Messiah. She recalls that this great God is equally faithful to all his people. He is the one who fills our emptiness with his fulness; who meets our innermost needs with satisfaction.

Lord Jesus,
This Christmas
As I sing the familiar carols
Hear the familiar readings
And ponder on familiar mysteries
Give to me the gift of pure worship:
That ability which Mary had
Of attributing to you
Your true worth
Your full value
Your inestimable greatness.
Teach me to be reverent.
Yet teach me how to express
The love that burns within my heart
As I think of your goodness to me:
That you have come to be
The light in my darkness
The hope in my despair
The strength in my weakness
The shelter in the storm
Yes
And my Saviour.

Elizabeth's son is born

Mary stayed with Elizabeth for some three months before returning to Nazareth. Just imagine the feelings of excitement and anticipation in those three people: the old priest who had prayed for years that a miracle would happen; the elderly woman who now carried a child whom God clearly was blessing from the time of his conception, and the young girl who marvelled daily at the privilege God was giving her – of becoming the mother of his own Son. Luke describes the events surrounding the safe arrival of God's miracle baby, and how Zechariah's speech is returned when they name the baby John.

'His first words were to thank God. The neighbours were awe-struck at this, and all these incidents were reported in the hill-country of Judaea. People turned the whole matter over in their hearts, and said, "What is this child's future going to be?" For the Lord's blessing was plainly upon him.
Then Zechariah, his father, filled with the Holy Spirit and speaking like a prophet, said...
"And you, little child, will be called the prophet of the most high, for you will go before the Lord to prepare the way for his coming. It will be for you to give his people knowledge of their salvation through the forgiveness of their sins. Because the heart of our God is full of mercy towards us, the first light of Heaven shall come to visit us – to shine on those who lie in darkness and under the shadow of death, and to guide our feet into the path of peace."'

Luke 1:64-67, 76-79

The father of a newborn child once tried to capture for me the emotions he felt as he watched his first child being born. 'It was a miracle,' he said. 'Wonderful. This baby is God's baby.'

Zechariah and Elizabeth knew, too, that John the Baptist, as he was to be called, was God's baby. His mission was to prepare the way for Jesus.

Father, as I think of John the Baptist and his
mission: to herald your coming and to urge
people to prepare their hearts to receive you,
new longings stir within my heart:

> *make me watchful*
> *keep me faithful*
> *bring me to repentance*
> *give me love*

that in love and with joy I may encounter you
anew and welcome you afresh when
Christmas Day dawns once more.

Mary's secret is revealed to Joseph

After three months away in the hills, Mary had to return to Nazareth and explain to Joseph that she was pregnant. We are not told precisely how Joseph felt on hearing this news. What does seem clear is that he was unable to accept that his bride-to-be was pregnant 'by the Holy Spirit.' It would appear that he believed that Mary had been unfaithful to him.

Unlike Mary, Joseph had no one with whom to share his pain and perplexity and shame. At that time, betrothal was absolutely binding. It could only be terminated by divorce. Unfaithfulness after betrothal was considered to be adultery and adultery was a legitimate reason for divorce. And so Joseph, on discovering Mary's pregnancy, decided to act within his legal rights and to break off the relationship, as privately as possible.

> 'But while he was turning the matter over in his mind an angel of the Lord appeared to him in a dream and said, "Joseph, son of David, do not be afraid to take Mary as your wife! What she has conceived is conceived through the Holy Spirit, and she will give birth to a son, whom you will call Jesus ('the Saviour') for it is he who will save his people from their sins."'
>
> Matthew 1:20-21

Although we might not have put such great store by a dream these days, for Joseph it would have seemed both a normal and powerful method through which God would communicate his plans. God's dream-vision so set Joseph's mind at rest that he replaced thoughts of instant divorce with plans for an immediate marriage. In this way Joseph provided both Mary and the unborn Jesus with the most effective moral support and protection he could possibly give – even though this must have been at cost to himself and despite wagging, gossiping tongues.

Did Mary lurch from fear to faith
From despair to hope
From doubt to belief
Dear Lord?
Or did she remain calm and serene
While Joseph mistrusted her?
You do not tell us
But the assurance you do give
Is that you were there
In the pain
Caring
And sharing
And making your purposes plain.
When friends ill-treat me,
Keep me trusting in your faithfulness
And in your ability to speak,
To vindicate,
And to restore.
So that your perfect purposes
May be fulfilled in me
As much as in Mary.

The birth of Jesus

When God had prepared both Mary and Joseph for the miracle which was about to take place – the birth of his Son – he ensured that the baby would arrive in Bethlehem, the place where the prophets had long ago foretold that the Messiah would be born of a virgin mother. At the beginning of his Gospel Luke describes how Jesus came to be born in Bethlehem and traces the events leading up to the birth.

Mary... gave birth to her firstborn, a son.
Luke 2:7

The journey from Nazareth to Bethlehem was eighty miles – not the kind of donkey ride most pregnant women would relish. Travellers took their own food on such a journey and were offered only the most primitive of accommodation. When Mary and Joseph arrived in Bethlehem they found the tiny town already overcrowded. That was why the Saviour of the world made his entry into the world in a common cave. And that was why his crib was the animals' feeding-trough.

There has never been a time when I have not accepted with my head that Jesus, God's Son, was born in a humble cave in Bethlehem. But it was not until I visited the Holy Land for myself that I grasped fully this fact with my heart.

I remember the moment of revelation well. It happened in the crypt of the Church of the Nativity in Bethlehem: the church which has been built over the spot where it is believed that Jesus was born.

In the crypt I allowed my eyes to grow accustomed to the dim light. In the candlelight I noticed a nun in one corner praying silently. But before I could collect my thoughts and begin to pray myself, a group of tourists came in. At first, their noisy enthusiasm irritated me and I was further annoyed when the leader of their party suggested that, though it was April and not December, they should sing 'Away in a Manger'. But as these tourists began to sing the familiar words –

Away in a manger, no crib for a bed
The little Lord Jesus laid down his sweet head
The stars in the bright sky looked down where he lay
The little Lord Jesus asleep on the hay

– I listened, gazing at the spot where the manger is supposed to have stood, and to my utter amazement tears began to trickle down my face. These tears, I knew, were tears of awe and wonder. Deep within me a certainty had taken root. God really had sent his Son to earth. It had happened here in Bethlehem. And he had come as a baby: dependent, wanting and needing to be found and touched and held and loved by those among whom he lived.

'When peaceful silence lay over all, and night had run half of her swift course, your all-powerful word, O Lord, leaped down from heaven from the royal throne.'
The Weekday Missal

> Thou who was rich beyond all splendour,
> All for love's sake becamest poor;
> Thrones for a manger didst surrender,
> Sapphire-paved courts for stable floor.
> Tho who wast rich beyond all splendour,
> All for love's sake becamest poor.
>
> Thou who art God beyond all praising,
> All for love's sake becamest Man;
> Stooping so low, but sinners raising
> Heavenwards by Thine eternal plan.
> Thou who art God beyond all praising,
> All for love's sake becamest Man.
>
> Thou who art love beyond all telling,
> Saviour and King, we worship Thee.
> Immanuel, within us dwelling,
> Make us what Thou wouldst have us be.
> Thou who art love, beyond all telling,
> Saviour and King, we worship Thee.
> Frank Houghton

Why, Lord, Why?
Why did you exchange the spaciousness of heaven
And the warmth of your Father's presence
For the squalor of a manger on earth
And the limitations of life as a man?
Why did you who made the heavens
The mountains
The stars
The sun
Strip yourself of your glory
To become a helpless, homeless baby?
Why did you come here
To this spot
To Bethlehem?

I came, my child, because I love you
I have always loved you
I will always love you
I came to rescue you from the clutches of the Evil One
To deliver you from sin
To be your Saviour
To bring you into the spaciousness I enjoy.
And I came as the prophets foretold:
To Bethlehem
To a woman's womb
To indwell you as I indwelt her
To become
Emmanuel
God with you and God in you.

Shepherds and angels rejoice

In Palestine, when a baby was born, local musicians congregated at the house to greet his arrival into the world with simple music. Since Jesus was born in a stable, this ceremony could not have been carried out. Even so, there was no absence of music when God's Son made his entry into the world. On the contrary, a vast army of angels made the music at this royal, yet humble birth. Luke records the lyric and attempts to capture the ecstasy:

> 'There were some shepherds living in the same part of the country, keeping guard throughout the night over their flock in the open fields. Suddenly an angel of the Lord stood by their side, the splendour of the Lord blazed around them, and they were terror-stricken. But the angel said to them,
> "Do not be afraid! Listen, I bring you glorious news of great joy which is for all the people. This very day, in David's town, a Saviour has been born for you. He is Christ, the Lord. Let this prove it to you: you will find a baby, wrapped up and lying in a manger."
> And in a flash there appeared with the angel a vast host of the armies of Heaven, praising God, saying,
> "Glory to God in the highest Heaven! Peace upon earth among men of goodwill!"'
>
> Luke 2:8-14

The shepherds, still dazzled by the brilliance of the angelic choir, somehow made their way up the terraced slopes of Bethlehem to the cave where the newborn baby lay. The sight of the baby – God in a manger – changed their lives. They returned to their work of shepherding overflowing with wonder and praise and awe.

Loving Father, this Christmas, like the shepherds, I would bow in awed wonder before the majesty of heaven revealed in the form of a baby. Fill me afresh with love as I contemplate these mysteries. Reveal yourself to me so that, like the shepherds and the angels, my heart may be filled with joy. And transform me so that this Christmas I may become more and more like this Christ-child I worship: ready to do your will in everything, even at cost to myself.

Hark, the heralds angels sing,
'Glory to the new-born King,
Peace on earth, and mercy mild,
God and sinners reconciled!'
Joyful, all ye nations, rise,
Join the triumph of the skies,
With the angelic host proclaim,
'Christ is born in Bethlehem.'

Hark, the herald angels sing,
'Glory to the new-born King.'

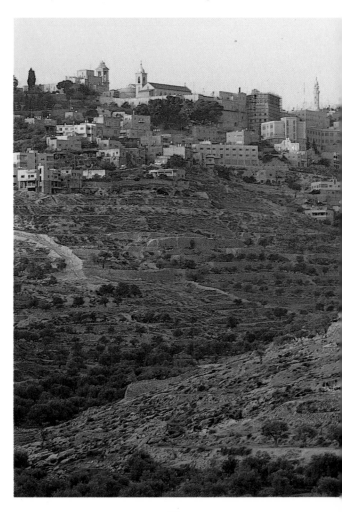

Christ, by highest heaven adored,
Christ, the everlasting Lord,
Late in time behold Him come,
Offspring of a virgin's womb.
Veiled in flesh the Godhead see;
Hail, the incarnate Deity,
Pleased as Man with man to dwell,
Jesus, our Immanuel!

Hark, the herald angels sing,
'Glory to the new-born King.'

Mary meditates

In the midst of all the excitement of the events of the first Christmas – the message of the angels, the visit of the shepherds – there is a still, quiet figure. Luke describes how 'Mary treasured all these things and turned them over in her mind'.

Since that time, thousands of people have attempted to do what Mary did: to contemplate the mystery of God becoming man. Many people have written down the fruit of their meditations but none more powerfully than the apostle John:

> 'When the world had its beginning, the Word was already there; and the Word was with God; and the Word was God. This Word was in the beginning with God. He was the agent through whom all things were made; and there is not a single thing which exists in this world which came into being without him. In him was life and the life was the light of men; and the light shines in the darkness, because the darkness has never been able to conquer it... The Word became a person, and took up his abode in our being, full of grace and truth; and we beheld his glory, glory such as an only son receives from his father... No one has ever seen God. It is the unique one, he who is God, he who is in the bosom of the Father, who has told us all about God.'
>
> John 1:1-5, 14, 18

These verses sum up for John his conviction that Jesus was the Word of God. Words tell us who people are, what people are like. Words are about communication and can lead us to understanding. Jesus is the Word of God because, having a unique intimacy with the Father, he alone is qualified to show us who God is and what he is like.

'The child that lies in the manger, helpless and abandoned to the love of His creatures, dependent entirely upon them to be fed, clothed and sustained, remains the Creator and Ruler of the universe.'

Thomas Merton

Lord God of hosts
I believe
Yet I struggle to understand.
Can it really be true?
You
The generous giver of being
The creator of the universe
The sustainer of all that is
Lie helplessly in a manger
Restricted by swaddling clothes
Limited by our humanity
Rejected by those you came to rescue
With nowhere to call your home?
I know it's true:
You became little and weak
That I might become great and strong
You allowed yourself to be bound in swaddling
cloth
That I might be unbound from the fetters of
death
You made your entry to earth
That I might gain access to heaven.

For this miracle of love
Living Lord God
I give you humble but heartfelt thanks and
praise.

John reflects on Christ's coming

The significance of Jesus' birth and life and death is the focus of the opening chapters of John's Gospel. He tells us God needed to send his Son into the world:

> '(Jesus) was in the world, and, although the world was made by him, the world did not recognize him. It was into his own home that he came, and yet his own people did not receive him. To all those who did receive him, to those who believe in his name, he gave the right to become the children of God.'
>
> John 1:10-12

The Jews were a privileged people: a chosen people. It was to the Jewish nation that God chose to send his Son. The tragedy was that this nation whom God loved failed to recognize the Lord of the Universe and, in their ignorance, rejected God's own Son.

What blinded their eyes? We know that they were looking for a conquering king to rescue them from the tyranny of the Romans. Was that why they failed to recognize their Messiah in the baby lying in Mary's arms? Or was it God's seeming ordinariness that proved the chief stumbling block: the incongruity of God in the squalor of a stable; God, the son of a Nazarene carpenter and a poor peasant girl? We shall never know why so many people rejected the Saviour of the world when he came. What we can be certain of is the truth of John's claim that if we believe in him and receive him, we may count ourselves as children of God, brothers and sisters of this child in the manger.

'To believe in Jesus means to take Jesus at his word, to accept his commandments as absolutely binding, to believe without question that what he says is true.

'For John, belief means the conviction of the mind that Jesus is the Son of God, the trust of the heart that everything he says is true and the basing of every action on the unshakeable assurance that we must take him at his word. When we do that we stop existing and begin living. We know what Life with a capital 'L' really means.'

William Barclay

O omnipotent God, who cares for each of us as if no one else existed and for all of us as if we were all but one! Blessed is the person who loves You. To You I entrust my whole being and all I have received from You. You made me for Yourself, and my heart is restless until it rests in You.

St Augustine

What can I give him, poor as I am?
If I were a shepherd, I would bring a lamb.
If I were a wise man, I would do my part,
Yet what I can, I give him,
Give my heart.

Christina Rossetti

The light of the world

As one year ends and we recall its tragedies and as another year unfolds and we look into the great unknown, it is easy to imagine that chaos reigns. But John assures us that in this tiny baby in Bethlehem a light which will never be extinguished has shone out upon our world:

> 'There emerged a man sent from God whose name was John. He came as a witness, in order to bear witness to the light, that through him all might believe. He himself was not the light; his function was to bear witness to the light. He was the real light, who, in his coming into the world, gives light to every man.'
>
> John 1:6-9

John the Baptist was like a candle in the darkness. But when Jesus came, the world was bathed in the light because he is:

God of God
Light of Light

The light which no darkness, however menacing, will be able to snuff out, the light which beams onto chaos and creates order and beauty, the light which illuminates our path. Jesus, the light of the world, is the one whose arrival the prophets promised:

> 'The people walking in darkness
> have seen a great light;
> on those living in the land of the
> shadow of death
> a light has dawned...
> For to us a child is born,
> to us a son is given,
> and the government will be on his shoulders,
> And he will be called
> Wonderful Counsellor, Mighty God,
> Everlasting Father, Prince of Peace.'
>
> Isaiah 9:2,6

Light shining in the darkness, light that is the light of men,
Light from the beginning, shining brightly now as then.
People rejoice, the night is gone,
God's redeeming work begun
In the birth of his Son.

Love come to dwell among us, love made flesh for every man,
Love from the beginning, our divine creator's plan.
People rejoice, the chains of sin
Which have bound you, God has broken
Through the death of his Son.

Life full of truth and beauty, life as it was meant to be,
Life from the beginning and into eternity.
People rejoice, dance and sing.
Worship Jesus, Lord and King,

Light shining in the darkness.

Anne Johnson, Paul Herrington and David Stone

Lord Jesus Christ,
Sun of righteousness
Shine upon us
Scatter the darkness from our path
And grant us peace
Joy
And everlasting life.

'I said to the man who stood at the gate of the year: "Give me a light that I may tread safely into the unknown." And he replied: "Go out into the darkness and put your hand into the hand of God, that shall be to you better than light and safer than a known way." '

Minnie Louise Haskins

Jesus is named

Certain ceremonies followed the birth of a baby boy in Palestine at the time when Jesus was born. One was circumcision. On the eighth day after his birth, a baby boy would not only be circumcised, he would also receive his name. So sacred was this ceremony that it would take place even if the eighth day happened to fall on the Sabbath. Another ancient ceremony was the purification after childbirth.

When a woman had given birth to a boy she was thought to be unclean for forty days. During this time she was not allowed to enter the Temple or to take part in any religious ceremony. At the end of forty days, she was required to bring to the Temple as an offering, a lamb and a pigeon. If she could not afford the lamb, she was allowed to bring 'the offering of the poor' – two pigeons – instead. It was the offering of the poor which Mary brought, as Luke reminds us:

'On the eighth day, when it was time to circumcise him, he was named Jesus, the name the angel had given him before he had been conceived.'

Luke 2:21

The name given to Jesus is of great significance. The root is the Hebrew word 'yasha' which means 'to bring into a spacious environment', 'to be at one's ease', 'to be free to develop without hindrance', 'salvation', 'wholeness'. Jesus came to give us all of these luxuries: to give us the freedom to become the people he always intended we should be and yet to give us the security of his never-ending love. He came to pour love in where there was no love.

But he also came to 'save' us from the consequences of going our own way, not God's way, of spoiling the perfect relationship he intended us to have with him, our Creator, with other people, and with his creation.

It was because humankind had broken God's 'rule' that Jesus came down to earth as a baby, lived as a man and died a criminal's death. He knew that we faced the death penalty – eternal separation from God – because of this broken relationship. He was concerned both that justice should be done and that we should be rescued. And so he stripped himself of his glory and exchanged it for the poverty of earth where he took upon himself the punishment which should have been ours. He is the Saviour of the world.

Lord Jesus, as I embark on yet another year
And with this reminder of your supreme
sacrifice
Rising before my eyes
I give you myself afresh
Take me as I am
Take me where you will
Do with me what you will
This New Year
And always.

Simeon's song

At the time when Jesus was born, hopes of the coming of the Messiah ran high. Most people believed he would come with pomp and ceremony to rescue Israel from its enemies. But a few thought differently. These were known as 'The Quiet in the Land'. They did not dream of violence or power or armies. Rather, they devoted themselves to a life of quiet prayer and constant watchfulness and waited patiently for the time when God would send the promised Saviour. Among these praying people was Simeon:

'Now there was a man in Jerusalem called Simeon, who was righteous and devout. He was waiting for the consolation of Israel, and the Holy Spirit was upon him. It had been revealed to him by the Holy Spirit that he would not die before he had seen the Lord's Christ. Moved by the Spirit, he went into the temple courts. When the parents brought in the child Jesus to do for him what the custom of the Law required, Simeon took him in his arms and praised God, saying:

"Sovereign Lord, as you have promised,
you now dismiss your servant in peace.
For my eyes have seen your salvation,
which you have prepared in the sight of all people,
a light for revelation to the Gentiles
and for glory to your people Israel."

'The child's father and mother marvelled at what was said about him. Then Simeon blessed them and said to Mary, his mother: "This child is destined to cause the falling and rising of many in Israel, and to be a sign that will be spoken against, so that the thoughts of many hearts will be revealed. And a sword will pierce your own soul too." '

Luke 2:25-35

According to Simeon, not only Jews but Gentiles also would benefit from the birth of Jesus and enjoy salvation through him. Simeon predicts that Jesus' life will demand a response from people. They will either be for him or against him. And he tells Mary the privilege of being God's mother will prove to be a costly one.

Christ our Saviour, from the Father,
Born for ever, only Son
You were there before creation
With the Father always one.

Dazzling brightness of the Father
Day-bright hope for all mankind
May the prayers of all your faithful
Through the world your favour find.

Jesus born of virgin mother
Praise to you this holy day
With the Father and the Spirit
Reign as one eternally

Prinknash Abbey

*Lord Jesus, I marvel at the prayerfulness of
Simeon which brought him into the kind of
stillness where your voice is clearly heard. And
I marvel at the quiet trust displayed by Mary
as, step by step, your will for her Son was
revealed. As this new year unfolds, grant to me
that quiet trust which is prepared to watch
and to wait, to listen and to believe in you at
all times and in all places.*

Anna thanks God for Jesus

'There was also a prophetess, Anna... She was very old;
she had lived with her husband seven years after her
marriage, and then was a widow until she was eighty-
four. She never left the temple but worshipped night
and day, fasting and praying. Coming up to them at that
very moment, she gave thanks to God and spoke about
the child to all who were looking forward to the
redemption of Israel.'

Luke 2:36-38

If Anna was married in her early teens, the custom in those days, she had been a widow for over sixty years by the time she saw the Christ-child for herself. Those who have lost a loved one often find that God is so real to them in their loss that they give themselves to him in a new way. It would appear that this had happened to Anna. Far from becoming an embittered widow, she had dedicated the whole of her life to prayer and fasting. And now her faithfulness was rewarded as she saw for herself the child who was to be the Saviour of the world.

John in his Gospel tells us that Jesus 'came to his own but his own did not receive him.' In Simeon and Anna we see two people who not only received him, but welcomed him, found joy in him and encouraged others to believe in him.

Anna's story shows us again that God comes to us as we go about our normal, daily tasks and that he also comes powerfully and unforgettably to those who keep silence before him.

Lord Jesus, I would worship you as Anna did,
in spirit and in truth.
Like her I would
submit all my nature to you,
that my conscience may be quickened by your
holiness,
my mind nourished by your truth,
my imagination purified by your beauty.
Help me to open my heart to your love
and to surrender my will to your purpose.
Like Anna
May I lift my heart to you
in selfless adoration and love.

An adaptation of a prayer by George Appleton

Arise, shine, for your light has come,
And the glory of the Lord has risen,
O arise, shine, for your light has come,
And the glory of the Lord is upon you.

You shall see and be radiant with joy!
Your heart shall thrill and rejoice,
And you shall know that I am the Lord,
Your Saviour, the Holy One of Israel.

Guided by a star

Christ came!
Christ comes!
Christ will come again!

This is the message of Advent and Christmas. When Jesus came to earth as a baby, God made sure that all sorts of people knew he was coming. Matthew tells us how 'wise men' as far away as Persia discovered the secret of the Messiah's miraculous birth. They came to the capital, Jerusalem, looking for an infant king. Herod's advisers tell him that it is in Bethlehem that 'the Christ' will be born.

'Then Herod invited the wise men to meet him privately and found out from them the exact time when the star appeared. Then he sent them off to Bethlehem saying, "When you get there, search for this little child with the utmost care. And when you have found him come back and tell me – so that I may go and worship him too."
The wise men listened to the king and then went on their way to Bethlehem. And now the star, which they had seen in the east, went in front of them as they travelled until at last it shone immediately above the place where the little child lay. The sight of the star filled them with indescribable joy.
So they went into the house and saw the little child with his mother Mary. And they fell on their knees and worshipped him. Then they opened their treasures and presented him with gifts – gold, incense and myrrh.
Then, since they were warned in a dream not to return to Herod, they went back to their own country by a different route.'

Matthew 2:7-12

These wise men, or Magi as they are sometimes called, were professional astrologers who had been trained to read the language of the sky. We do not know quite what they saw in the heavens to tell them that a king had been born in Palestine. What we do know is that some heavenly brilliance assured them that a new 'king' had made his entrance into the world. So here again we see God speaking powerfully to people who are going about their normal everyday tasks – even when that task is to read the signs of the stars.

These wise men from the East seem to have been driven to
Bethlehem by an instinctive yearning to worship the new king
for themselves and to lay at his feet the most priceless gifts
they could think of: gold, incense and myrrh.

All-powerful Father,
you have made known the birth of the Saviour
by the light of a star
May he continue to guide us with his light
Enlighten us with his radiance
And strengthen us with his care
Until, with joy,
He takes us to our eternal home.

The Weekday Missal

Heartache and joy

Simeon warned Mary that the arrival of Jesus into the world
would bring heartache as well as joy. People would have to
make up their minds about him. Some would respond to him
with dedicated and adoring love. Others would hate and reject
him.

Mary did not have long to wait before the truth of this
prophecy dawned on her. Matthew describes how Jesus'
existence posed a threat to Herod, the king, and how this
triggered off brutality and violence:

'Herod issued orders, and killed all the male children of
two years and under in Bethlehem and the surrounding
district – basing his calculation on his careful
questioning of the wise men.'
Matthew 2:16

'Here is a terrible illustration of what men will do to get rid of
Jesus Christ. If a man is set on his own way, if he sees in Christ
someone who is liable to interfere with his ambitions and
rebuke his ways, then his one desire is to eliminate Christ; and
then he is driven to the most terrible things, for then, if he does
not break men's bodies, he will break their hearts.'

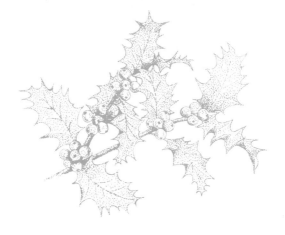

Father, with this account of Herod's hatred of you ringing in my ears, it would be easy to point the finger at him and to deny that seeds of distrust, anger and violence germinate in my heart too. Thank you that this sobering story jars – jolts me out of my complacency and disturbs me enough to want to ensure that my life is dedicated afresh to you. May I mean, take seriously, and go on to live the words that I pray:

Almighty God,
give me grace to cast away the works of darkness
and to put on the armour of light,
now in the time of this mortal life,
in which your Son Jesus Christ
came to me in great humility:
so that on the last day,
when he shall come again in his glorious majesty
to judge the living and the dead,
I may rise to the life immortal;
through him who is alive and reigns
with you and the Holy Spirit,
one God, now and for ever.

The Alternative Service Book 1980 (adapted)

This is our God
The Servant King
He calls us now
To follow Him
To give our lives
As a daily offering
Of worship to
The Servant King

Graham Kendrick

The test of love

While Herod was doing his worst, trying to ensure that Jesus was murdered in the massacre of the infants, God was at work. He warned Joseph, in a dream, to take Mary and Jesus into Egypt, well out of Herod's reach.

'But after Herod's death an angel of the Lord again appeared to Joseph in a dream and said, "Now get up and take the infant and his mother with you and go into the land of Israel. For those who sought the child's life are dead."
So Joseph got up and took the little child and his mother with him and journeyed towards the land of Israel. But when he heard that Archelaus was now reigning as king of Judaea in the place of his father Herod, he was afraid to enter the country. Then he received warning in a dream to turn aside into the district of Galilee and came to live in a small town called Nazareth – thus fulfilling the old prophecy, that he should be called a Nazarene.'

Matthew 2:21-23

Joseph's unquestioning obedience to every instruction given to him by God stands in stark contrast to Herod's fear and barbarism. This sounds a fitting note on which to end these meditations on 'the comings of Christ'. Christ came. Christ comes. Christ will come again. And when he comes, he will look for those who are as obedient to him as Joseph was:

'Obedience is the one certificate of a Christian character.'
Andrew Murray

'If you really love me
you will keep the commandments I have given you...
Every man who knows my commandments and obeys them
is the man who really loves me.'
Jesus

Heavenly Father,
As this New Year unfolds,
Enlarge my vision of yourself
Deepen my trust in your love
Increase my faith in the perfection of your
purposes
That when you speak
I may listen
And obey
With the glad assurance
That you will never cause your child
A needless tear.

Text copyright © 1987 Joyce Huggett
This edition copyright © 1987 Lion Publishing

Published by
Lion Publishing plc
Icknield Way, Tring, Herts, England
ISBN 0 7459 1121 8 (paperback)
ISBN 0 7459 1332 6 (casebound)
Lion Publishing Corporation
1705 Hubbard Avenue, Batavia, Illinois 60510, USA
ISBN 0 7459 1121 8 (paperback)
Albatross Books Pty Ltd
PO Box 320, Sutherland, NSW 2232, Australia
ISBN 0 86760 898 6 (paperback)

First edition 1987

Acknowledgments

Cover illustration by Ann Plowden
Text illustrations by Paul Granger

Photographs by Susanna Burton, day 34; Alistair Duncan, day 37;
Sonia Halliday Photographs: Sonia Halliday, days 21, 28, 35,
Else Trickett, day 1; The Hutchison Library, day 7; ITC Entertainment Ltd:
Jesus of Nazareth, day 24; Lion Publishing: David Alexander, days 23,
27, David Townsend, day 18; Jon Willcocks, day 13; Rex Features, days 8,
16; John Span, day 15; Peter Stiles, day 10; ZEFA (UK) Ltd, days 3, 5, 31.

Bible quotations from *Good News Bible*, copyright 1966, 1971 and 1976
American Bible Society, published by the Bible Societies/Collins;
Holy Bible, New International Version (British edition), copyright 1978
New York International Bible Society; *The New English Bible*, second
edition, copyright 1970 Oxford and Cambridge University Presses;
The New Testament in Modern English, copyright 1960 J.B. Phillips;
Revised Standard Version, copyright 1946 and 1952, second edition
1971, Division of Christian Education, National Council of the Churches
of Christ in the USA.

Extracts from *The Alternative Service Book 1980* are reproduced by
permission of the Central Board of Finance; extracts from *The Weekday
Missal* are reproduced by permission of Collins Liturgical Publications.

Other copyright quotations are reproduced by kind permission of the
publishers: Metropolitan Anthony of Sourozh, *Living Prayer*, published
and © 1980 by Darton, Longman and Todd Ltd, London/Templegate
Publishers, Illinois, day 3; William Barclay, *Daily Study Bible,
The Gospel of John, Volume 1*, The St Andrew Press, days 21, 30;
John Bunyan, *Pilgrim's Progress*, Penguin, day 14; Michael Green,
I Believe in Satan's Downfall, Hodder & Stoughton Ltd, day 12;
Matthew Henry, *Commentary on the Whole Bible*, Marshall Pickering,
day 13; Anne Johnson, Paul Herrington and David Stone, *Light Shining
in the Darkness*, from the cassette and songbook *King of Kings*,
Ears and Eyes Music, day 31; Eric Marshall and Stuart Hample,
Children's Letters to God, Collins Publishers, London/Simon and
Schuster Inc, New York, Introduction; Thomas Merton, *Meditations on
the Liturgy*, Darton, Longman & Todd Ltd, day 18 and *Seeds of
Contemplation*, Anthony Clarke Publishers, day 29; E. Milner-White,
My God, My Glory, SPCK, day 6; Toki Miyashina, *Psalm 23 - An
Anthology*, The St Andrew Press, day 18; Andrew Murray, *Humility:
The Beauty of Holiness*, Marshall Pickering, day 37; Trina Paulus,
Hope for the Flowers, Paulist Press, day 9; Michel Quoist, *Prayers of
Life*, Gill and MacMillan, day 19; John Tauler, *The Perfection of Love*,
Collins Publishers, day 20; Stephen Travis, *The Jesus Hope*, Word
Books, day 6.

Every effort has been made to trace and contact copyright owners. If
there are any inadvertent omissions in the acknowledgments, we
apologize to those concerned.

Printed and bound in Spain